# This Book Belongs To



..........................................................................

..........................................................................

..........................................................................

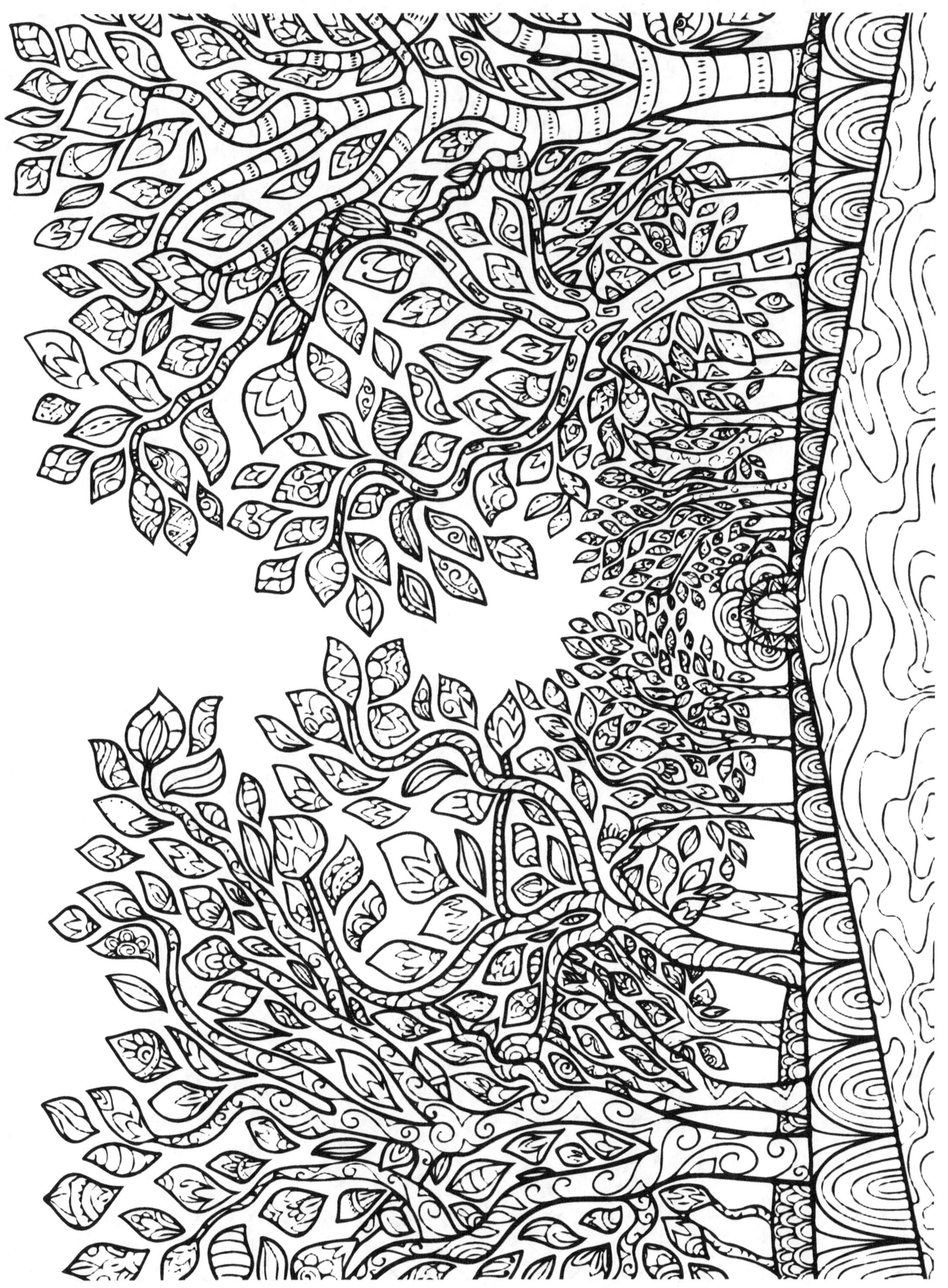

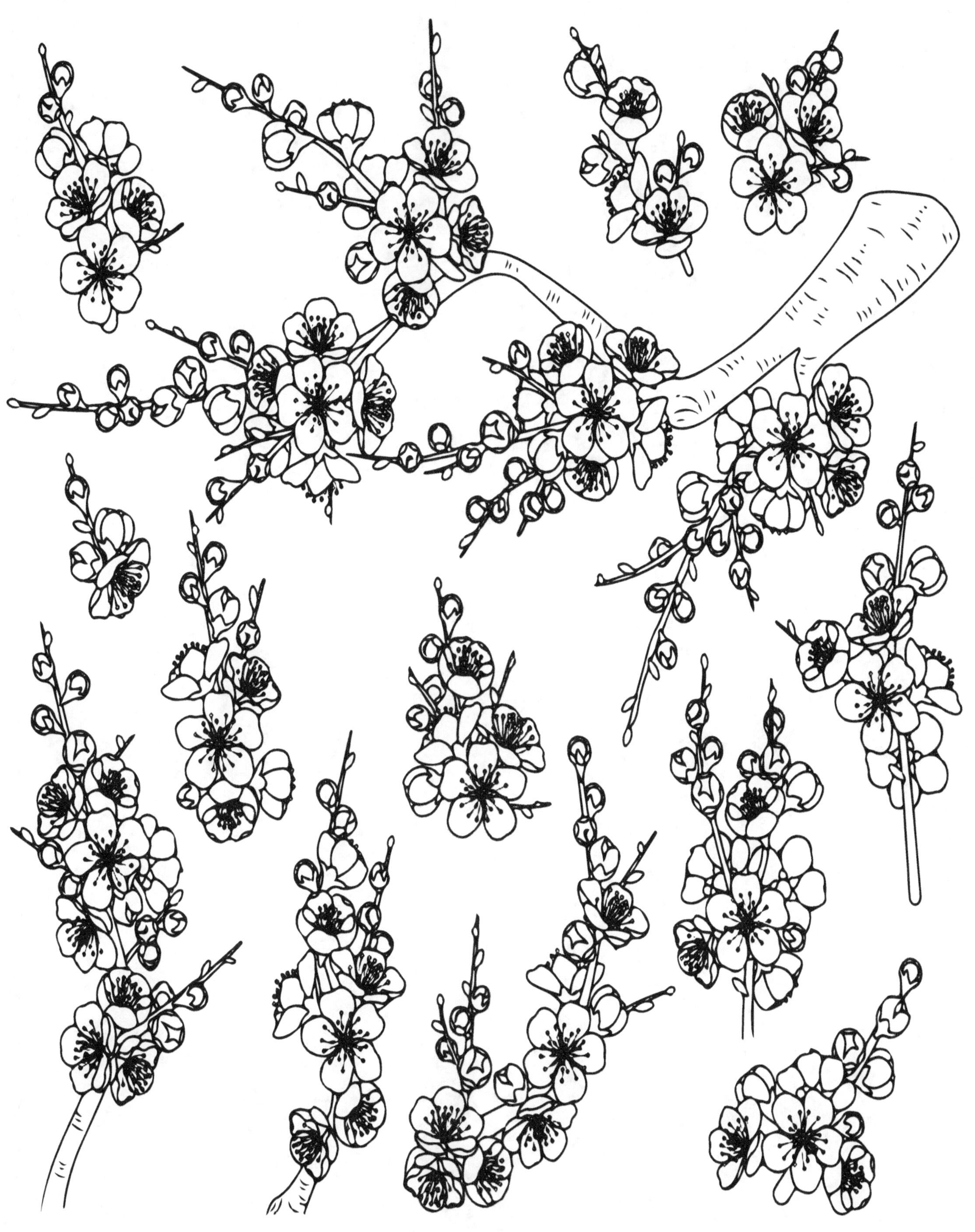

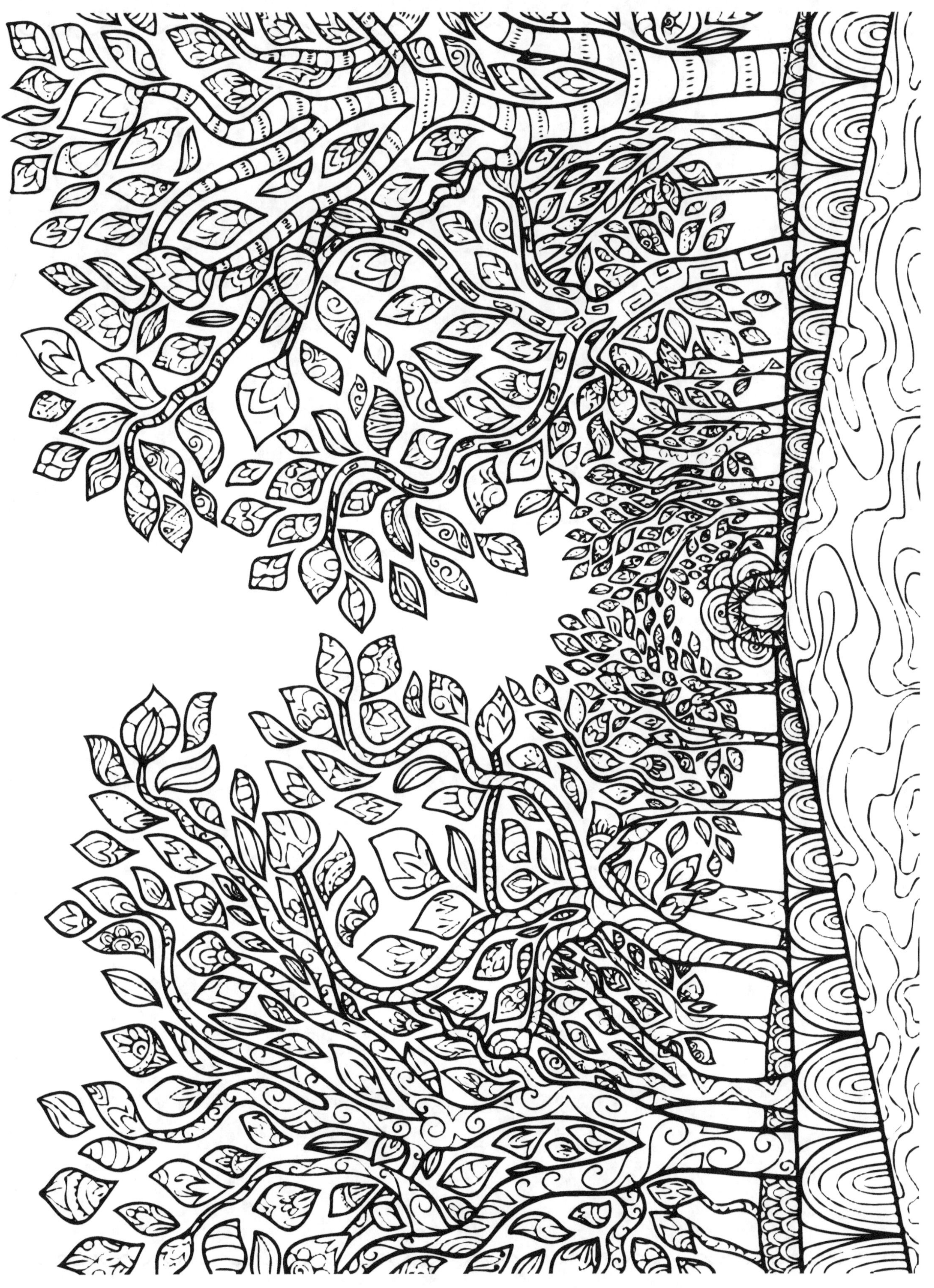

www.ingramcontent.com/pod-product-compliance
Lightning Source LLC
Chambersburg PA
CBHW081024260726
48662CB00026B/3092